THE OFFICIAL
RANGERS
ANNUAL 2013

Written by Douglas Russell

Designed by Brian Thomson

A Grange Publication

© 2012 Published by Grange Communications Ltd., Edinburgh, under licence from Rangers Football Club. Printed in the EU.

Photography © Rangers Football Club.

ISBN 978-1-908925-14-5

£7.99

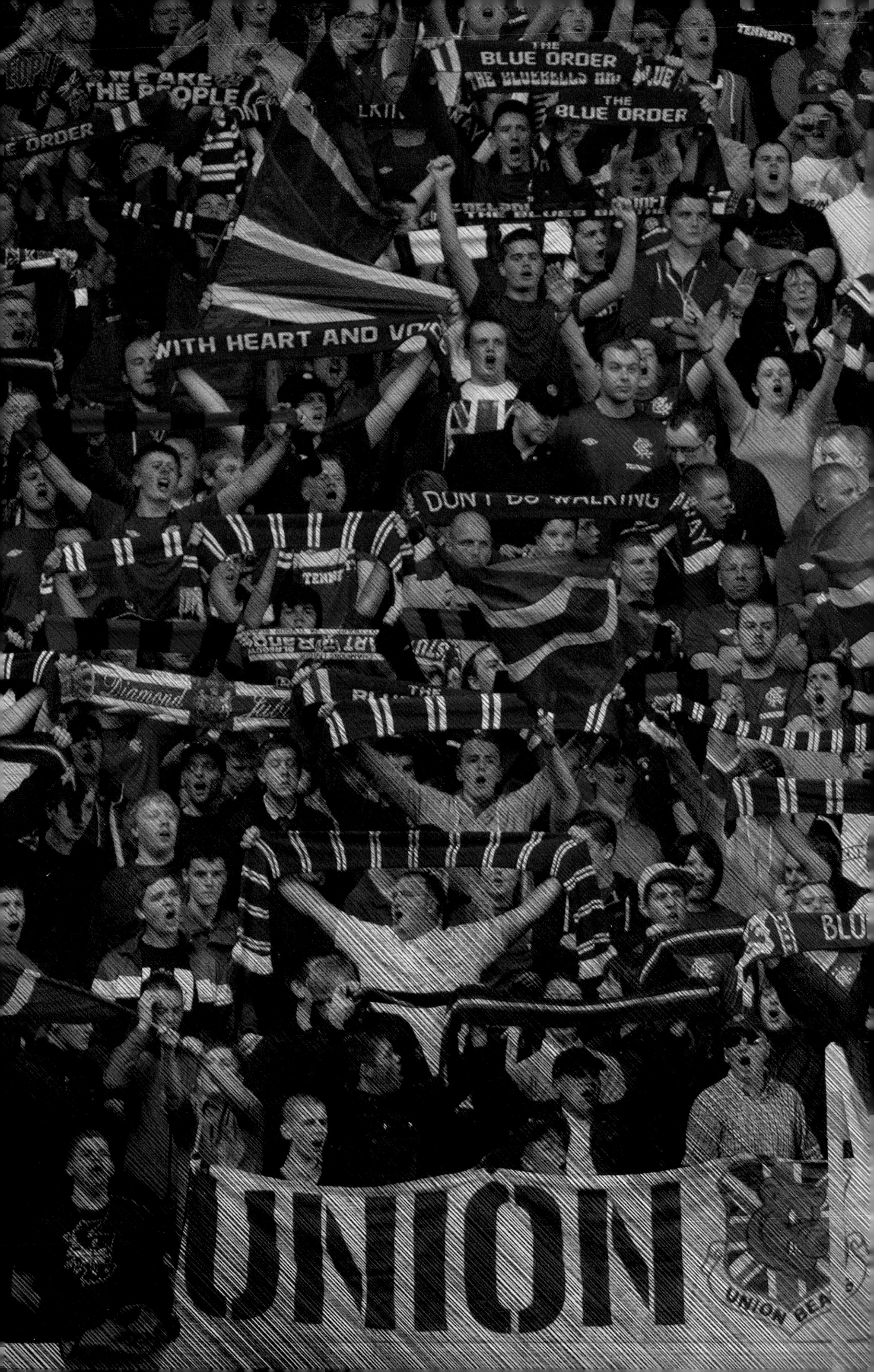
THE BLUE ORDER
WE ARE THE PEOPLE
THE BLUE ORDER
UNION

CONTENTS

A TO Z OF RANGERS
(PART 1)

A is for **Lorenzo Amoruso** who, on a glorious afternoon at Celtic Park in May 1999, became not only the first Rangers captain to secure the championship at the home of the Club's greatest rivals but also the first foreign player to skipper Rangers to a league title. **Dick Advocaat** was the Club's first manager from overseas and in his first season after arriving from Holland, he led Rangers to a domestic treble in 1998/99.

B is for **Baxter**, maybe the most naturally talented Ibrox player of them all. Excelling in the heat of the Old Firm inferno, **Jim Baxter** was only on the losing side twice in 18 encounters with the team in green between 1960 and 1965. In the Scottish Cup final replay of 1963 which Rangers won 3-0, his domination of the midfield helped ensure one of the most one-sided clashes against Celtic for many a long year. He played alongside the penalty box predator **Ralph Brand** who became the first footballer to score in three successive Scottish Cup finals when Rangers defeated Dundee 3-1 in April 1964. **Brand** actually netted six times in seven cup finals for Rangers and was never on a losing side in a domestic final. Defender **Terry Butcher** arrived in Scotland at the start of the Souness era in 1986 and several months later, netted the goal in a 1-1 draw against Aberdeen at Pitttodrie that confirmed Rangers first title win in nine years.

LORENZO AMORUSO

C is for Cooper. First and foremost a Rangers man, **Davie Cooper** was a winger of supreme ability and one of the Club's most gifted sons. In the 1979 Drybrough Cup final, he scored one of the greatest goals ever seen at Hampden when he juggled past four bemused Celtic defenders before netting Rangers third in a 3-1 win. **Davie Cooper** tragically passed away in March 1995, just a few days after his 39th birthday. **Eric Caldow** was an exceptionally fast full back who captained both Rangers and Scotland in the late 1950s and early 1960s. Winner of five league championship medals, **Caldow** missed only two Scotland internationals in the period from April 1957 to April 1963 before sadly breaking a leg during a game against England at Wembley in the latter year.

D is for both **Dawson** and **Durrant**. **Jerry Dawson** 'Prince of Goalkeepers' was the last line in defence in the 1930s/1940s and won five League Championships, two Scottish Cups, two Scottish War Cups, two Summer War Cups and one Southern League Cup during his 16 Ibrox years. Govan boy **Ian Durrant** joined the only team he ever wanted to play for as a schoolboy and, following the arrival of Graeme Souness as manager, made the No. 10 jersey virtually his own. The abiding image of the player, arms aloft in 'Victory V' celebration after scoring, is now part of Rangers folklore.

E is for the **European Cup Winners' Cup** which the team lifted in May 1972 after defeating Moscow Dynamo 3-2 at Barcelona's Nou Camp Stadium. Goals from Colin Stein and Willie Johnston (a double) started the celebrations. This was the third time that Rangers reached the ultimate stage of this competition, having been beaten in previous finals by Fiorentina (1961) and Bayern Munich in 1967.

F is for all the **Fergusons** who have worn the blue over the years. Long before his managerial success at Manchester United, **Alex Ferguson** was a centre forward who scored 19 goals in 29 league appearances in Season 1967/68. Midfielder **Ian Ferguson** is one of only three Rangers players to have every medal from the '9 in a Row' sequence of championship success. **Barry Ferguson**, another midfielder, always led by example and was a true fans' favourite. In Season 2002/03, he netted 18 goals and captained the side to a domestic treble of League Championship, Scottish Cup and League Cup.

BARRY FERGUSON

PAUL GASCOIGNE

G is for **Greig**, the greatest-ever Ranger, who played over 850 games during his 18 years at the Club. In addition to skippering the side to European glory in 1972, **John Greig** is the only Rangers player to have won three separate trebles – in 1963/64, 1975/76 and 1977/78. **Richard Gough** was another great captain and the most successful since the days of Davie Meiklejohn some 60 years earlier. Brave as a lion, the defender amassed nine League Championship medals, three Scottish Cup medals and six League Cup medals. The season after **Gough** was appointed captain, manager Walter Smith brought **Andy Goram** to Rangers from Hibernian. 'The Goalie' would become an Ibrox legend. Walter Smith also lured the wayward genius **Paul Gascoigne** to Glasgow. At the end of his first season, a stunning hat-trick against Aberdeen in late April 1996 confirmed championship flag number 46.

JOHN GREIG

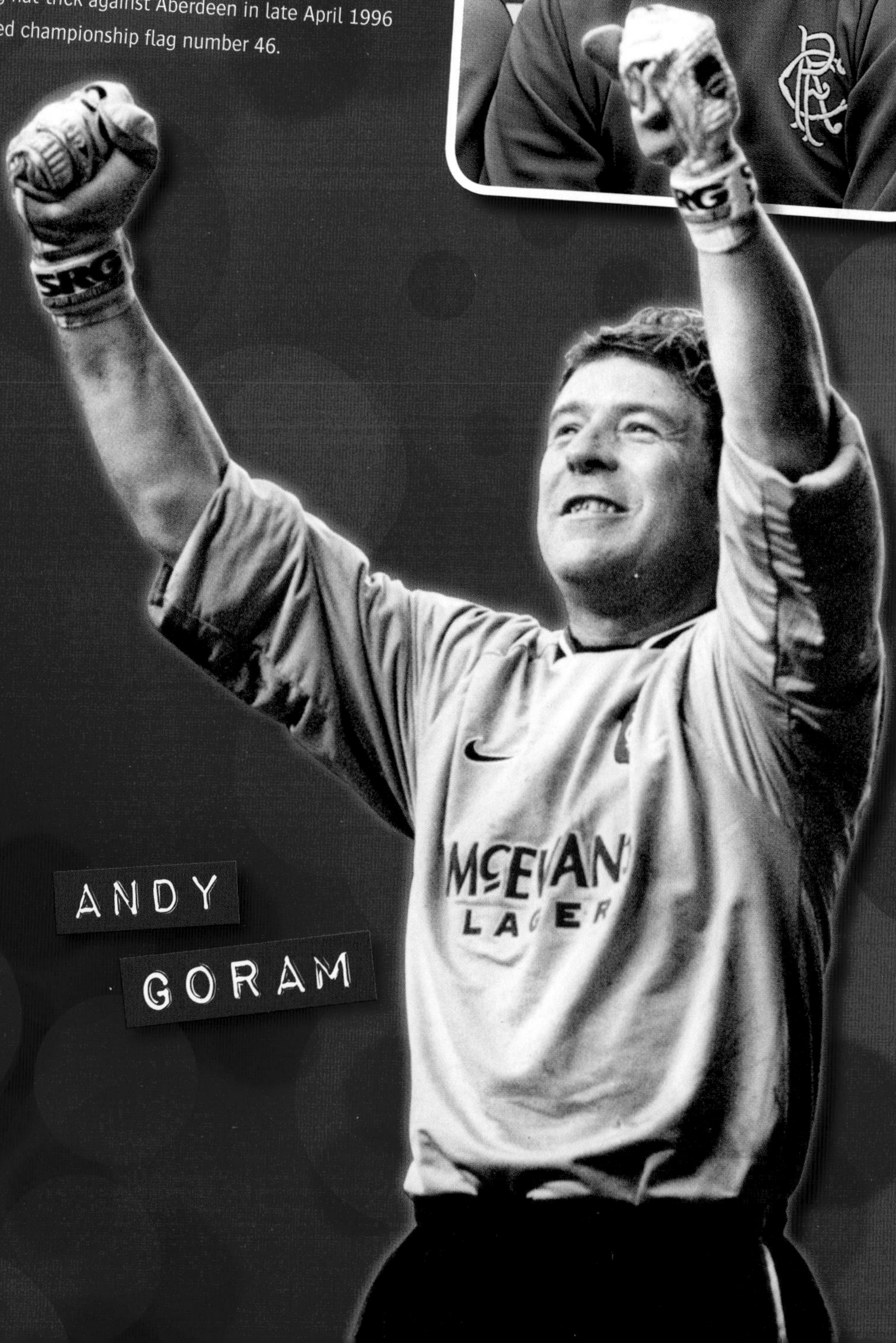

ANDY GORAM

RICHARD
GOUGH

MARK
HATELEY

H is for **Henderson** and **Hateley**. Back in the 1960s, winger **Willie Henderson** was one of the true characters of the Scottish game and his superb crosses were food and drink to forwards Ralph Brand and Jimmy Millar. **Mark Hateley**, the most feared striker in Scotland at one time, scored two of Rangers most famous goals of the modern era – the opening goals against Aberdeen in Glasgow on championship day 1991 and against Leeds United at Elland Road in the European Cup campaign of Season 1992/93.

I is naturally for **Ibrox Stadium**. With its imposing red brick façade, the Main Stand was officially opened on New Year's Day 1929 when visitors Celtic were beaten 3-0. Following the disaster in 1971 when 66 Rangers fans lost their lives, three new stands were then built and opened in August 1979 (Copland Road Stand), August 1980 (Broomloan Road Stand) and December 1981 (Govan Stand) with the completion of the Club Deck, on top of the Main Stand, in 1991.

Continued on Page 30...

U17s GLASGOW CUP FINAL 16 APRIL 2012
Rangers 1 Celtic 1
(Rangers won 4-2 on penalties)

Fraser Aird in action

Charlie Telfer in action

Captain Andy Murdoch with the Glasgow Cup

Darren Ramsey in action (left), and celebrating his equalising goal (below).

Liam Kelly celebrates after saving two penalties in the shoot-out

THE LEAGUE CHAMPIONSHIPS

When Rangers won the SPL championship on the last day of Season 2010/11, it was the Club's 54th league flag. Here's a brief history of the record-breaking total.

Pictured: Paul Gascoigne

Season 1890/91

Rangers shared the first-ever Scottish Football League Championship with Dumbarton (following a 2-2 play-off draw) after both teams ended the actual campaign on 29 points.

Season 1898/99

Winning every league game, Hibernian were 10-0 casualties along the way. Schoolteacher RC Hamilton hit 21 goals in the 18 league games.

Season 1899/1900

The title was taken seven points ahead of Celtic and the season included impressive 7-0, 6-0 and 6-1 victories against Clyde, Dundee and Kilmarnock respectively.

Season 1900/01

Three in a row with the Club's Old Firm rivals again second but this time six points adrift.

Season 1901/02

To win the championship, Celtic required five points from five games at one stage but a 4-2 Rangers victory at Parkhead in January turned the tide.

Season 1910/11

With the league campaign now 34 games, Celtic's six year domination was brought to an end. Centre forward Billy Reid hit 38 goals in 33 appearances.

Season 1911/12

The championship was won by six points from Celtic. During this season, because of a national coal strike, Rangers actually supplied the fuel for a train to take them to Kirkcaldy for a match against Raith Rovers!

Season 1912/13

Four points behind Celtic with 14 games to play, the Light Blues went on an unbeaten run to take the title.

Season 1917/18

Before the final game, both Old Firm teams had 54 points. Rangers then beat Clyde 2-1 and Celtic drew 1-1 at home against Motherwell.

Season 1919/20

A marathon league campaign of 42 games ended with 71 points (from a possible 84) and, for the first time, over a century of goals – 106 to be precise.

Season 1920/21

With Bill Struth now in charge, Rangers only dropped two points in the opening 23 league fixtures. Although Celtic won at Ibrox in January, it was to be their last victory in this corresponding fixture for 62 years!

Season 1922/23

Dane Carl Hansen became the first foreign player to net in an Old Firm clash – Rangers won 2-0 at Ibrox in January – and the Light Blues finished five points ahead of Airdrie.

Season 1923/24

Unbeaten until the 2-1 loss away to Ayr United in January, centre forward Geordie Henderson was top scorer (with 23 goals this time) for the second successive season.

Season 1924/25

Airdrie, for the third year in a row, pushed Rangers hard and with one game to go sat just one point behind. Henderson's strike rate was an even more impressive 27 league goals.

Season 1926/27

Title number 15 and Bob McPhail (230 Rangers career goals) arrived from Airdrie to form an outstanding left-wing partnership with Alan Morton, who some say was the finest footballer of his generation.

Season 1927/28

24 goals in the first six games and the team were on their way to equaling Celtic's record of 16 championships. Jimmy Fleming claimed 33 goals in 34 games.

Season 1928/29

Fleming hit 33 in 35 appearances in the season the new 10,000 seat Grandstand (Main Stand) was opened.

Season 1929/30

Bill Struth's all-conquering side won every tournament available to them - the League Championship, the Scottish Cup, the Glasgow Cup and the Charity Cup.

Season 1930/31

A Club record of five successive titles. Victory against Celtic in the Ne'erday clash set Struth's side off on an unbeaten twelve game run.

Season 1932/33

Motherwell (first, third and second in the previous three campaigns) again proved formidable but Rangers 3-1 Fir Park win in February was crucial.

Season 1933/34

With 20 goals in the first four games – Jimmy Smith scored 12 of them - Rangers ended this championship season with 118 in total. Smith's tally was 41 goals from 32 appearances.

Season 1934/35

In the opening game, Rangers crushed Dunfermline 7-1. Celtic's challenge was strong but a crowd of 83,000 viewed their 2-1 Ibrox January defeat as the beginning of their end in the title race. Incidentally, when Kilmarnock won 3-2 in Glasgow in December, it was Rangers first home league defeat in three years!

Season 1936/37

Aberdeen headed the queue of challengers but, right from the word go, Rangers showed consistency with a run of 17 games without a loss. Jerry Dawson, the prince of goalkeepers, was ever-present in the team.

Season 1938/39

Despite losing 6-2 to Celtic early-on, their Old Firm rivals were still left 11 points adrift when the trophy was being awarded to Rangers. Centre-forward Willie Thornton had now been joined by two other legends bearing the same Christian name – Waddell and Woodburn – in the last season before the outbreak of World War Two.

Season 1946/47

For the first post-war campaign, Hibernian became a force in the east and ended the period just two points adrift. Top scorers for Rangers were Jimmy Duncanson and Willie Thornton with 18 league goals each.

Season 1948/49

On the last day of the title race, leaders Dundee required one point at Falkirk to become champions. They lost and Rangers 4-1 away win at Albion Rovers confirmed the crown. The Ibrox men also became the first Scottish side to lift the domestic treble of League Championship, Scottish Cup and League Cup in the same season.

Season 1949/50

After drawing 0-0 with second placed Hibernian in the penultimate game, Rangers needed just one point from their last match. A 2-2 draw away to Third Lanark guaranteed just that. Of the famed 'Iron Curtain' defence, four members (Brown, Young, Cox and McCall) never missed a league game all season.

Season 1952/53

This year's title was won on goal difference from Hibernian after Willie Waddell's late equaliser against Queen of the South at Palmerston Park ensured a 1-1 draw in the final match.

Season 1955/56

Despite winning only one of their opening six league encounters, a 23 game unbeaten run meant celebrations in due course. Queen of the South lost 8-0 at Ibrox in the very first Scottish fixture to be played under floodlights.

Continued on Page 40...

THE MAGNIFICENT seven

Rangers scored seven goals against Celtic at Ibrox in the league last season.

Here's a reminder of the magnificent seven.

1

Steven Naismith
(4-2, 18 September 2011)

2

Nikica Jelavic
(4-2, 18 September 2011)

3

Kyle Lafferty
(4-2, 18 September 2011)

Steven Naismith
(4-2, 18 September 2011)

4

5

Sone Aluko (3-2, 25 March 2012)

7

Lee Wallace (3-2, 25 March 2012)

6

Andrew Little (3-2, 25 March 2012)

RANGERS LEGENDS QUIZ

Guess the identity of the 10 Rangers Legends from the clues below...

1. I was club captain at Hamburg before arriving at Ibrox. In addition to scoring the winner in the 1998 League Cup final, I netted from the penalty spot when Rangers secured the championship at Celtic Park in May 1999.

2. I joined Rangers at the tender age of 16 on a salary of £1 a week. I was the first post-war Rangers player to break the 100 goal barrier and, throughout my career, I was never once yellow carded or sent-off.

3. When I signed for Rangers, I was deputy-captain of England. Although not a natural goal-scorer, my headed strike against Aberdeen at Pittodrie in May 1987 has a special place in the history of the Club.

4. In reference to my full blooded tackling, my nickname was 'Captain Cutlass' at the Club and, during my Rangers career in the 1950s and 1960s, I once played 165 games in succession.

5. During my earlier days as a player, I changed clubs in January 1973 for a record transfer fee between English teams of £352,000. I eventually arrived at Ibrox in 1986 after two seasons in Italy with Sampdoria.

6. Before joining Rangers, I won a French league title with Monaco under the management of Arsene Wenger. Nicknamed 'Attila' during my Ibrox career, my goals against Aberdeen in May 1991 clinched championship number three of 9 in a Row.

7. Chelsea and Manchester United were just two of my previous clubs. At the end of my last game for Rangers in November 1989, I was given a standing ovation at Ibrox by 40,000 fans.

8. When Scotland crushed England 5-1 at Wembley Stadium in 1928, I was a member of the victorious dark blue team. That was the day when 'The Wee Blue Devil' became my nickname.

9. I joined Rangers from Tottenham in October 1987 when manager Graeme Souness agreed a record fee of £1 million. I was captain of the Club by the time that 9 in a Row was reached in 1997.

10. When Rangers defeated Morton 5-0 in the 1963 League Cup final, I scored four of the goals with my cousin Alec Willoughby netting the fifth. In Season 1963/64, I established a Club record that still stands of 57 goals in all competitions.

Answers on Page 61

RANGERS THEN • RANGERS NOW

EXIT 21

EXIT 21

RANGERS

• RANGERS FOREVER • EST. 1872

EXIT 22

FOREVER

THE TREBLES

When Rangers lifted all three domestic trophies of League Championship, Scottish Cup and League Cup in Season 2002/03, it was the seventh time in the Club's proud history that this special feat had been achieved. Here's a reminder of each of those magnificent campaigns:

2. SEASON 1963/64

Unbeaten in the section stage of the League Cup – Celtic suffered 3-0 defeats both home and away – second division Morton were hammered 5-0 in the final of the competition. Cousins Jim Forrest and Alec Willoughby shared the goals between them with Forrest claiming four (a cup final record for a Rangers player) and his relative the other.

Kilmarnock pushed Rangers hard in the league and indeed led the race at one point in the campaign. However, their challenge virtually ended following a 2-0 Glasgow defeat in mid-March as manager Scot Symon's side headed for a third championship in four seasons.

With Partick Thistle (3-0), Celtic (2-0) and Dunfermline (1-0) all failing to halt the team's Scottish Cup progress, approximately 121,000 gathered at Hampden for the Rangers/Dundee clash in April. In one of the truly great Scottish Cup finals, the Ibrox men left it late to snatch victory but, after two goals in the last two minutes, the destination of the trophy was settled following a 3-1 victory. Ralph Brand, one of the scorers that day, became the first player to score in three successive Scottish Cup finals.

final – manager Bill Struth's team became the first-ever Scottish side to secure the treble two seasons later. Although the section stage of the League Cup started badly with draws against Clyde and Hibernian as well as a 3-1 Old Firm defeat in the east end of Glasgow, results improved and, in what was the section decider, Celtic were beaten 2-1 at Ibrox in front of 105,000 fans. Later, on the final day in March, Rangers defeated Raith Rovers 2-0.

It was very much a two horse race in the league with closest rivals Dundee needing only a point in the last game at Falkirk to claim the title. They lost and, with Rangers 4-1 victory at Stirling Albion, the championship trophy returned to the Trophy Room.

The Scottish Cup final – a 4-1 win against Clyde - was played the week before the above league encounter. One of the scorers that day was Billy Williamson who was making his first Scottish Cup appearance of the season. In the same competition the previous year, he netted the winner in the 1-0 win over Morton. Amazingly, that too had been his first Scottish Cup appearance of the season!

3. SEASON 1975/76

After disposing of Queen of the South and Montrose in the quarter-final and semi-final of the League Cup respectively, Celtic provided somewhat tougher opposition in the October final. One goal decided the game – a flying header by midfielder Alex MacDonald that ignited the blue touchpaper at one end of the national stadium.

In the championship, Jock Wallace's men went on an unbeaten run from early December until the end of the campaign with the Celtic clash at Ibrox near the start of this sequence proving crucial. Prior to this game, Rangers Old Firm rivals were three points ahead but a 1-0 win (Derek Johnstone scored) narrowed the gap at the top of the table. The league title was eventually secured against Dundee United at Tannadice – Derek Johnstone again bagged the only goal of the game but this time in the first minute – with Celtic six points behind in second place.

Seven days later, the treble was complete when Hearts lost 3-1 in the Scottish Cup final. Derek Johnstone once again netted right after kick-off to record a rather unique double of first minute goals in trophy-deciding games in successive weeks!

4. SEASON 1977/78

This season's League Cup final was also against Celtic and ended 2-1 after extra-time. Gordon Smith and Davie Cooper scored for Rangers. Following a previous 6-1 win against Aberdeen in the same competition, their manager Billy McNeill suggested this was the best display of football he had ever witnessed by an Ibrox side.

Indeed it was the team from the north of the country who proved to be closest rivals in the league race, having defeated Rangers in three of the four championship encounters. However, one point ahead with three games remaining, Rangers won all their remaining fixtures to take the crown. Earlier, in the initial Old Firm game of the season, Celtic led 2-0 at half time but a superb second period of three goals by Rangers turned the match on its head.

Maybe not surprisingly, it was Aberdeen who contested the trophy on Scottish Cup final day. Rangers totally dominated the game even if the close 2-1 score fails to convey the fact. With two trebles in just three years, Jock Wallace's side became legends.

5. SEASON 1992/93

Fifteen years on it was Aberdeen once again offering the toughest domestic opposition and, for the fourth time in six years, the Granite City side jousted with Rangers in the final of the League Cup. Walter Smith's side lifted the trophy with a 2-1 win in extra time.

Showing remarkable consistency, Rangers went on a tremendous run in the league and, after losing 4-3 away to Dundee early-on in the league championship in August, lost only once before clinching the title against Airdrie at Broomfield in May. With Ally McCoist and Mark Hateley top scorers on 34 and 21 respectively, the team ended the campaign nine points in front of second place Aberdeen.

The team in red then joined the champions at Celtic Park – Hampden was being renovated – to contest the Scottish Cup final but returned north empty-handed again following another 2-1 defeat.

6. SEASON 1998/99

Number six of the seven was just a wee bit more special. The first part of the treble was confirmed when St Johnstone (also Scottish Cup semi-final opponents later in the season) lost 2-1 in the final of the League Cup at Celtic Park. The scorers that day were French striker Stephane Guivarc'h and German midfielder Jorg Albertz.

Since the formation of the Scottish League over 100 years previously, a Rangers side had never won the championship at the home of their greatest rivals but, on 2 May 1999, that is exactly what Dick Advocaat's side achieved at Celtic Park. The game, a fiery and controversial clash, was won 3-0 with Neil McCann (a double) and Jorg Albertz the goal heroes. Captain Lorenzo Amoruso also entered the record books as the first foreign player to skipper Rangers to Scotland's top domestic honour.

The Scottish Cup final at the new Hampden also involved Celtic but this time the game was a more subdued affair with striker Rod Wallace claiming the only goal of the game.

7. SEASON 2002/03

Alex McLeish joined the ranks of the great Rangers managers when he led the Club to this domestic treble. Goals from Claudio Caniggia and Peter Lovenkrands against Celtic in the League Cup final at Hampden ensured triumph number 23 in this competition. The Dane had now scored the winner in the last two cup finals against Celtic.

In the closest league race for many years, the destination of the flag was still in doubt right up to the final whistle of the last game of the season and came down to goal difference between the Old Firm giants. With Rangers beating Dunfermline 6-1 at Ibrox, the tally of 101 goals scored and 28 goals conceded (as opposed to Celtic's 98 and 26 respectively) was just enough for the celebrations to begin.

It was fitting that Lorenzo Amoruso, who had been immense all season, should hit the winner against Dundee six days later in the Scottish Cup final as the Italian defender was playing his last game for the Club before moving to the Premiership. It was the perfect end to a perfect day of another perfect season.

Francisco Sandaza

SPOT THE DIFFERENCE

Spot the 7 differences in the classic picture below...

A.

B.

Answers on Page 61

A TO Z OF RANGERS

(PART 2)

J is for **Johnstone** and **Jardine**. At just 16 years old, **Derek Johnstone** became the youngest player to score the winning goal in a cup final when his header at Hampden against Celtic brought the League Cup – Rangers first silverware in four years – back to the Trophy Room in October 1970. Just like **Johnstone**, defender **Sandy Jardine** was a member of the side that triumphed in Europe in 1972 and indeed scored the opener in the 2-0 semi-final win against tournament favourites Bayern Munich. Jardine played over 670 games for Rangers, collecting three championship and five Scottish Cup medals along the way.

K is for **Kitchenbrand**, a striker from South Africa who scored 24 goals in 25 league games in 1955/56. He famously hit five goals past Queen of the South that season during the very first Scottish League match to be played under floodlights.

L can only be for **Laudrup**, the Danish superstar who graced the Ibrox turf for three glorious years. It was **Brian Laudrup's** flashing header at Tannadice in May 1997 that confirmed championship number nine of 9 in a Row. One year earlier, he dismantled Hearts at Hampden in the final of the Scottish Cup when he scored twice and created the other three in a 5-1 triumph.

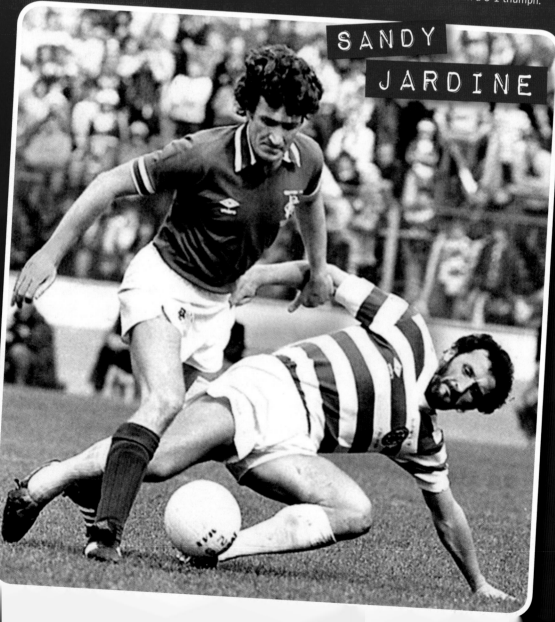

SANDY JARDINE

ALLY MCCOIST

M is for **Moses McNeil**, one of the founding fathers of Rangers in 1872 and also the Club's first international player when he was capped for Scotland in 1876.

During his illustrious career as a player, **Ally McCoist** was never less than super and scored a record 355 goals for Rangers and won Europe's Golden Boot award in consecutive seasons - 1991/92 and 1992/93. In the first of those campaigns, he reached a career total of 200 league goals whilst in 1992/93 he hit 34 goals in 34 championship games before breaking his leg in Portugal on duty with Scotland. He was the Club's leading scorer in nine of his fifteen seasons at Ibrox. As manager, he was the guiding light during the dark days of 2012.

Fiery midfielder **Alex MacDonald** scored the winner against Celtic in the final of the League Cup in October 1975, the first leg of domestic treble success that season. Very few players could distribute a football with the uncanny accuracy of winger **Tommy McLean** who was a member of the same team.

The superbly gifted **Ian McMillan**, dubbed 'the wee prime minister' because of both the way he controlled the game and the Prime Minister at the time Harold McMillan, played alongside Jim Baxter in what many consider to be one of Rangers finest-ever teams back in the early 1960s.

As manager, **Alex McLeish** led his players to a domestic cup double in his first season in charge followed by a memorable treble in 2002/03, the following year.

Govan born **Davie Meiklejohn** was at Rangers from 1919 to 1936 (playing 635 games) and scored the crucial opening goal (a penalty) against Celtic in the 1928 Scottish Cup final when Rangers ended their 25 year hoodoo in this competition. Although not the regular penalty taker, defender **Meiklejohn** felt that, as captain, the responsibility was his. The rest, as they say, is history.

Also in the team that day was the finest footballer of his generation, winger **Alan Morton** whose oil portrait takes pride of place above the splendid marble staircase inside the main entrance at Ibrox Stadium.

31

GEORGE NIVEN

N is for goalkeeper **George Niven** who was carried off with a head injury in the first half of the 1953 Scottish Cup final. Returning for the second period swathed in bandages – after stitches both outside and inside his ear – he was outstanding. During his Rangers career of five championships, two Scottish Cups and one League Cup, ex-miner **Niven** fractured arms, wrists, fingers, shoulders and his jaw!

O is for the **Osasuna Bull**, a Spanish gift of porcelain and one of the many fascinating items on display in the Ibrox Trophy Room. Opened in 1959 to house the growing treasure trove of silverware and memorabilia, the Trophy Room remains the crowning glory of the stadium.

P is for **Parlane** and **Provan**, striker and full back respectively. **Derek Parlane** netted the Club's 6000th league goal on the day that he scored all four in a 4-2 victory against Hearts in January 1975. Defender **Davie Provan**, a superbly balanced player equally at home in either full back position, was at Rangers from 1958 to 1970 and spent five patient years in the reserves awaiting his chance in the first team.

Q is for **the Queen's cousin Princess Alexandra** who, in May 1973, was the first member of the royal family to attend the Scottish Cup final when Rangers defeated Celtic 3-2 in front of nearly 123,000 spectators. This was the last final in Scotland to be played before a six figure crowd.

R is for the duo of **Russell** and **Roberts**. **Bobby Russell** exuded midfield class and memorably scored the winner in Holland on the night that PSV Eindhoven were beaten at home for the very first time in European competition in Season 1978/79. The Rangers cause was all that mattered to defender **Graham Roberts** and despite barely two seasons in Glasgow from 1986 to 1988, the Englishman is still revered down Govan way.

S is for four managers with the surnames of **Struth, Symon, Souness** and **Smith**. Their records are as follows: **Bill Struth** (1920-1954) – 18 League Championships, 10 Scottish Cups and 2 League Cups; **Scot Symon** (1954-1967) – 6 League Championships, 5 Scottish Cups and 4 League Cups, **Graeme Souness** (1986-1991) – 3 League Championships and 4 League Cups and **Walter Smith** (1991-1998, 2007-2011) – 10 League Championships, 5 Scottish Cups and 6 League Cups.

T is for **Tiger**. Winner of four league titles, three Scottish Cups and two League Cups, Club captain **Jock 'Tiger' Shaw** was 42 years of age when he retired as a Rangers player in 1954 following the Club's North American tour.

U is for the **UEFA Cup**, now known as the **UEFA Europa League**, a tournament Rangers first entered in Season 1982/83 with a first round 3-0 aggregate win over German side Borussia Dortmund. Rangers, of course, reached the **UEFA Cup** final in 2008 but lost 2-0 at the City of Manchester Stadium to Zenit Saint Petersburg, bossed by former Rangers manager Dick Advocaat.

WALTER
SMITH

V is for **Valletta** and **Vladikavkaz**, sides that both conceded 10 goals to Rangers in Europe. In 1990/91's European Cup, **Valletta** of Malta lost 6-0 and 4-0 over two legs. Then, in the same competition in Season 1996/97, Russian champions **Vladikavkaz** were defeated not only 3-1 at Ibrox but also 7-2 in front of their own fans. **Tom Vallance**, a founder member of Rangers, was captain for the Club's first nine seasons. The powerful full back also had paintings exhibited at the Royal Scottish academy!

W is for **Willie Waddell**, a winger who was an integral part of the great post-war side that dominated Scottish football in the late 1940s and the early 1950s. As manager, he guided Rangers to European glory in 1972. Another legendary manager was **Jock Wallace** who was at the helm when Rangers secured the clean sweep of domestic trebles in 1975/76 and 1977/78. Centre half **Willie Woodburn**, a member of the famed post-war 'Iron Curtain' defence, was a truly magnificent player whose game was virtually faultless. He also had a simple philosophy – nothing else mattered but Rangers success.

X is for ex Celt **Maurice Johnston** whose arrival at Ibrox in 1989 made all the headlines. The striker made nearly as many again three months later when he scored the only goal of the game in an Old Firm derby. Johnston went on to win two league titles, playing for the jersey as if to the manor born.

Y is for **George Young**. Winner of six League Championships, four Scottish Cups and two League Cups with the hugely successful post-war side, Club captain 'Corky' – he always carried a champagne cork for luck – also skippered Scotland 48 times in 53 international appearances.

Z is the final letter in the surname of **Jorg Albertz**. The German midfielder scored one of the most stunning of all Old Firm goals when, in January 1997, his blistering 30 yard free kick recorded a speed of 79.8 miles per hour before hitting the back of the net.

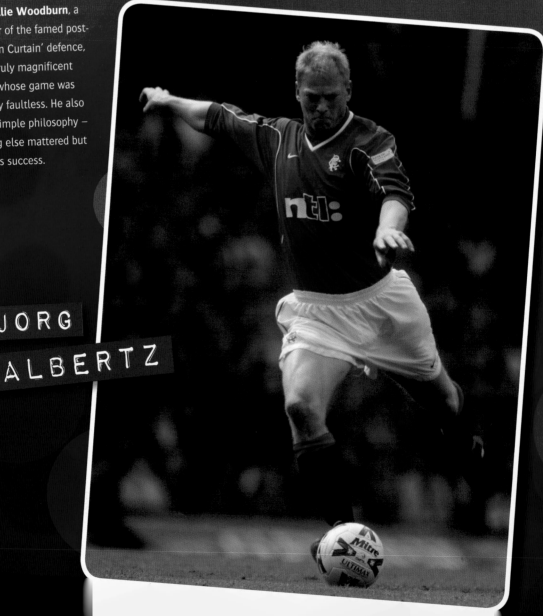

JORG ALBERTZ

JOCK WALLACE

GLORY
IN EUROPE

In 1961, Rangers became the first British club to reach the final of any European competition following an impressive run that saw Ferencvaros (Hungary), Borussia Mönchengladbach (Germany) and England's Wolverhampton Wanderers all fall by the wayside on the road to a Cup Winners' Cup final date with Fiorentina of Italy. The team from Florence proved too strong however winning 2-0 at Ibrox and 2-1 at home for an aggregate victory of 4-1.

It was a similar scenario in 1967 with more disappointment at the ultimate stage of the same competition when Bayern Munich won 1-0 in Nuremberg. The Light Blues had reserved their best form for the games leading up to the final with victories over Borussia Dortmund (the German holders), Real Zaragoza of Spain and the powerful Bulgarian side Slavia Sofia.

In Season 1971/72, Rangers faced Rennes of France in the first round of the European Cup Winners' Cup. After a 1-1 away draw - Willie Johnston netted for the visitors - midfielder Alex MacDonald scored the only goal of the game at Ibrox and manager Willie Waddell's side progressed to meet Sporting Lisbon of Portugal in the second round.

**Pictured: Willie Johnston
with the European Cup Winners' Cup**

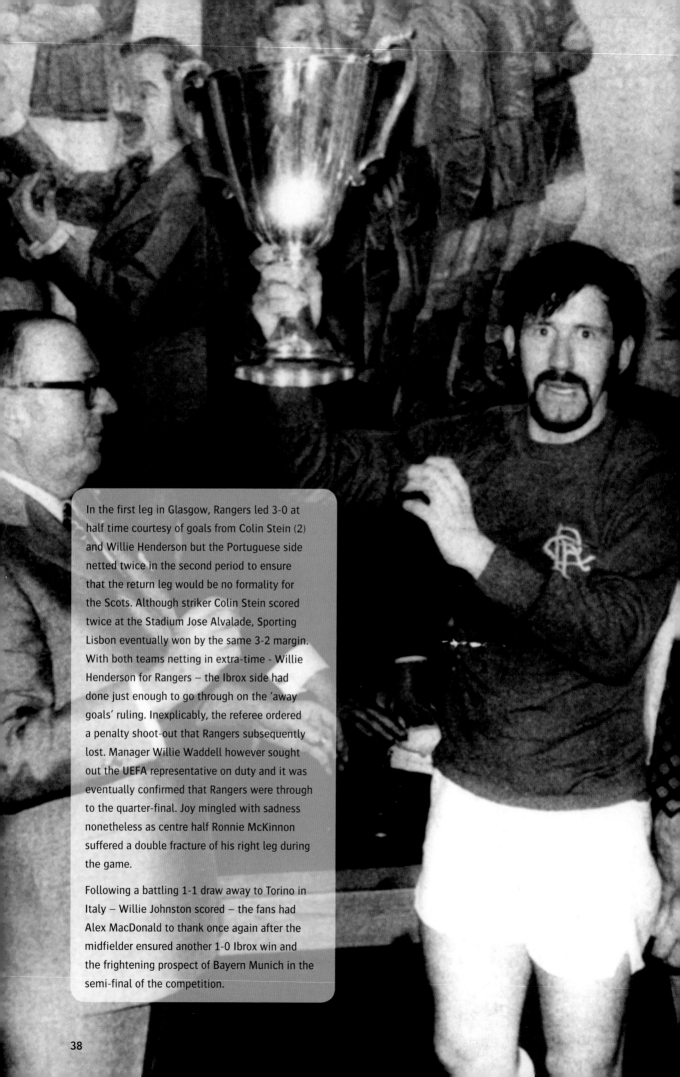

In the first leg in Glasgow, Rangers led 3-0 at half time courtesy of goals from Colin Stein (2) and Willie Henderson but the Portuguese side netted twice in the second period to ensure that the return leg would be no formality for the Scots. Although striker Colin Stein scored twice at the Stadium Jose Alvalade, Sporting Lisbon eventually won by the same 3-2 margin. With both teams netting in extra-time - Willie Henderson for Rangers – the Ibrox side had done just enough to go through on the 'away goals' ruling. Inexplicably, the referee ordered a penalty shoot-out that Rangers subsequently lost. Manager Willie Waddell however sought out the UEFA representative on duty and it was eventually confirmed that Rangers were through to the quarter-final. Joy mingled with sadness nonetheless as centre half Ronnie McKinnon suffered a double fracture of his right leg during the game.

Following a battling 1-1 draw away to Torino in Italy – Willie Johnston scored – the fans had Alex MacDonald to thank once again after the midfielder ensured another 1-0 Ibrox win and the frightening prospect of Bayern Munich in the semi-final of the competition.

...ghtening? Yes indeed as the German outfit included
...rld class talents such as Roth, Hoeness, Breitner,
...ier, Muller and the supremely gifted Franz
...ckenbauer in their ranks. Indeed, all six players
...uld be part of the German side crowned European
...mpions after defeating Russia 3-0 some weeks later.

...ce again however the continent brought out the
...t in Rangers as a 1-1 draw in Germany confirmed. A
...wd of 80,000 at Ibrox celebrated in the first minute
...he game when Sandy Jardine scored before young
...ker Derek Parlane added another first half goal to
...rantee passage into a third European final in just
... a decade.

...Nou Camp Stadium in Barcelona was the venue
...he 1972 European Cup Winners' Cup final between
...gers and Moscow Dynamo, the first Russian side to
...ar in the final of a European football competition.
...Scots dominated from the start and took the lead
...ay through the first period when Dave Smith's

through ball was swept home by Colin Stein. The cultur...
Smith was also involved in the second goal when, jus...
before the break, his cross into the box was headed
home by Willie Johnston. Four minutes into the seco...
half it seemed all over when Johnston scored again t...
make it 3-0 following a massive kick-out by keeper
Peter McCloy. However, after substitute Eschtrekov
pulled one back, the Soviets poured forward forcing
Rangers to defend resolutely. Three minutes from ti...
the pressure from the Russians paid off again and it...
was 3-2. In due course, the referee sounded the fin...
whistle, confirming that silverware of a non-Scottis...
variety would soon be carried up that famous marb...
staircase to the Ibrox Trophy Room.

Rangers: McCloy, Jardine, Mathieson, Greig, Johns...
Smith, McLean, Conn, Stein, MacDonald and John...

THE LEAGUE CHAMPIONSHIPS

(Continued from Page 17)

Pictured: Brian Laudrup

Season 1956/57

Although Hearts led for most of the journey, 11 wins and a draw in the remaining 12 games (including a vital 1-0 Tynecastle victory) meant that Rangers crossed the line two points ahead of the Edinburgh side. Centre-forward Max Murray hit 29 goals, almost a third of the team's 96 total.

Season 1958/59

Going into the final 90 minutes, Hearts were again close and only two points behind. Amazingly, relegation-threatened Aberdeen won 2-1 at Ibrox but Hearts also lost – at Celtic Park! The title was back for the third time in four seasons.

Season 1960/61

The championship was won on the last day of the season by one point from Kilmarnock when a 7-3 victory over their county rivals Ayr United grabbed the headlines. In the second game of that campaign, Celtic were crushed 5-1 in the east end of Glasgow.

Season 1962/63

This was the year of the big freeze and Rangers, after defeating Celtic 4-0 on New Year's Day, did not play another game until March 9. With a team comprising the likes of Ritchie, Shearer, Caldow, Greig, McKinnon, Baxter, Henderson, McMillan, Millar, Brand and Wilson, manager Scot Symon had built one of the truly great Rangers teams.

Season 1963/64

Old foes Celtic were beaten five times in five games as the period ended with the first domestic treble in fifteen years. It was the third championship in four years.

Season 1974/75

Jock Wallace's side ended nine years of Celtic dominance when Colin Stein's goal in the 1-1 draw against Hibernian meant not only a share of the points but also the league title. Of the 38,585 at Easter Road that day, over 30,000 were believed to be Rangers fans!

Season 1975/76

Unbeaten in the new 10 team Premier League from early December until the end of the campaign, Derek Johnstone scored the winner at Tannadice on championship day. This was another season of triple glory – the third in the Club's history.

Season 1977/78

In the opening Old Firm clash, Rangers were 2-0 down at the break but a second half revival (including two goals from Gordon Smith and one from Johnstone) secured a famous victory. A fourth domestic treble was also realised.

Season 1986/87

The arrival of Graeme Souness as player/manager transformed the Club. Despite being nine points behind Celtic at one stage, a 1-1 draw at Pittodrie in early May secured the point that guaranteed the championship flag.

Season 1988/89

The first leg of the 9 in Row journey was reached following the 4-0 defeat of Hearts at Ibrox. Kevin Drinkell, top scorer for the season, scored twice.

Season 1989/90

This was the year of Maurice Johnston. Although Trevor Steven netted the title-winning goal at Tannadice in April, former Celtic player Johnston was top scorer with fifteen. The side's January Old Firm win was the first in a Celtic Park derby for more than 20 years.

Season 1990/91

For the third season in a row, Aberdeen proved to be closest challengers and, indeed, required only one point at Ibrox on the last day of the season to claim the league crown. However, Mark Hateley's two goals in the game ensured legendary status for the player.

Pictured: Ally McCoist

Season 1991/92

'Golden Boot' winner Ally McCoist hit 34 of the record 101 goal total and Rangers won 19 of their 22 away league fixtures.

Season 1992/93

From late August until late March, 29 games passed without defeat. Ally hit another 34 goals as Rangers secured the Club's fifth domestic treble.

Season 1993/94

Mark Hateley, top scorer with 22 league goals, became the first Englishman to win the Football Writers' Player of the Year award.

Season 1994/95

Rangers led for most of the campaign and, by early March, were 15 points ahead of Motherwell in second place. By the end of April, the gap was 20 points.

Season 1995/96

Paul Gascoigne hit a hat trick against Aberdeen in the game that eventually decided the trophy's destination. The previous September, he scored a magnificent goal in the east end of Glasgow on the day that Celtic suffered their only league defeat.

Season 1996/97

9 in a Row was finally confirmed at Tannadice when Brian Laudrup's headed strike – the only goal of the game – ensured full points against Dundee United. The Dane had been sensational all season.

Season 1998/99

In over 100 years of Scottish League football, a Rangers team had never won the championship at the home of their greatest rivals but a 3-0 triumph at Celtic Park in May changed all that. Another domestic treble - the Club's sixth - was also registered.

Season 1999/2000

21 points ahead of Celtic by the end, this season included comprehensive away victories against Aberdeen (5-1), Motherwell (5-1) and Dundee (7-1) as well as excellent 4-2 and 4-0 Old Firm wins.

Season 2002/03

The closest league race for many years was decided on the last day of the season when Rangers defeated Dunfermline 6-1 at Ibrox to edge out Celtic on goal difference. Captain Barry Ferguson was immense throughout the whole league and cup campaign, leading the team to domestic supremacy and the Club's seventh treble.

Season 2004/05

Starting slowly, Rangers trailed Celtic by seven points after just five games. Alex McLeish's side kept believing however and famously reaped their reward on 'Helicopter Sunday' against Hibernian at Easter Road.

Season 2008/09

Once again the championship was decided on the last day of the league season when Rangers, with Walter Smith now back at the helm, turned on the style against Dundee United at Tannadice to record a 3-0 win.

Season 2009/10

Back-to-back SPL titles were achieved with three games to spare when Rangers defeated Hibernian 1-0. Unfortunately, due to the demolition of the old East Stand at Easter Road, only 1500 Rangers fans could be accommodated to witness this title triumph.

Season 2010/11

For the second time in three seasons, it was another 'last day' scenario and Rangers required victory at Rugby Park to retain the title. Walter Smith's side started like a whirlwind and virtually blew Kilmarnock away with three goals in the first seven minutes.

RANGERS ANNUAL:
GOAL OF THE SEASON 2011/12

In the opening Old Firm clash of the 2011/12 campaign, the first of four Rangers goals was scored by Steven Naismith when he bulleted home with a right foot strike from the edge of the area.

IBROX
STADIUM

SEASON 1989/90

The cultured Trevor Steven signed from Everton and ex-Celt Maurice Johnston arrived in somewhat sensational circumstances from Nantes. Both of these new signings would become major players for the Club as Rangers, despite losing their opening two league encounters, retained the championship for the first time since 1976. By the end of the campaign, Johnston was top scorer in the league with 15 goals, the most famous of which was probably his late winner when Celtic were beaten 1-0 at Ibrox in November. Incidentally, when Rangers recorded the same score at Celtic Park in early January, it was the Light Blues first 'Ne'erday' win at this ground in over twenty years! Midfielder Trevor Steven netted the title-winning goal against Dundee United at Tannadice in April.

SEASON 1989-90	P	W	D	L	F	A	Pts
Rangers	36	20	11	5	48	19	51
Aberdeen	36	17	10	9	56	33	44
Hearts	36	16	12	8	54	35	44

SEASON 1990/91

Striker Mark Hateley arrived from French side Monaco and by the end of his first year at the Club, the player had virtually achieved legendary status. In many ways, it was a difficult time in Govan early-on in the season – Terry Butcher left the Club under controversial circumstances, injuries to key players such as Richard Gough, Ian Ferguson, Ally McCoist and Trevor Steven disturbed the team pattern and, in April, Graeme Souness returned to Liverpool as manager at a time when the championship race was at a final crucial stage. On the last day of the league campaign, with Walter Smith now in charge, Aberdeen required only a draw with Rangers to claim the title. However, on one of the most dramatic Ibrox occasions for many a long year, two Hateley goals meant that the Light Blues lifted a

SEASON 1990/91	P	W	D	L	F	A	Pts
Rangers	36	24	7	5	62	23	55
Aberdeen	36	22	9	5	62	27	53
Celtic	36	17	7	12	52	38	41

Two new faces were goalkeeper Andy Goram (simply 'The Goalie' in due course) and midfielder Stuart McCall who joined from Hibernian and Everton respectively as the champions began their title defence with a 6-0 triumph against St. Johnstone in early August. Ally McCoist netted 34 times that season. As well as becoming the first Scot to win Europe's 'Golden Boot' trophy, the striker claimed his 200th Scottish League goal away to Aberdeen in early May. In total, Rangers had buried an astonishing 101 goals in 44 domestic league games. Certainly victory in 19 out of 22 away games went a long way to securing a fourth successive championship – for the first time in over 60 years! Incidentally, this period would realise the Club's first League and Scottish Cup double since 1978 following victory over Airdrie on the last day of the season at Hampden.

SEASON 1991-92	P	W	D	L	F	A	Pts
Rangers	44	33	6	5	101	31	72
Hearts	44	27	9	8	60	37	63
Celtic	44	26	10	8	88	42	62

SEASON 1992/93

After losing to Dundee at Dens Park in mid-August, Rangers showed remarkable consistency and were beaten in only one championship game before securing the league title away to Airdrie at the beginning of May the following year. Two players were responsible for 65 of the teams 97 goals – Ally McCoist (another special season for him) equalled his previous year's tally of 44 and Mark Hateley (by now a true blue warrior king) contributed greatly with 21 of his own. Rangers also won a first treble (the fifth in the club's history) since the managerial days of Jock Wallace back in 1977/78 in addition to embarking on the most wonderful European run. A series of 10 unbeaten Champions League games took

SEASON 1992/93	P	W	D	L	F	A	Pts
Rangers	44	33	7	4	97	35	73
Aberdeen	44	27	10	7	87	36	64
Celtic	44	24	12	8	68	41	60

SEASON 1993/94

With Celtic conspicuous by their absence in the top three, it had been the somewhat unlikely duo of Aberdeen and Motherwell offering the strongest championship challenge that season. Indeed, the Fir Park outfit defeated Rangers both home and away before the defending champions (despite losing the likes of Goram and McCoist for much of the campaign) made it 6-in-a-row. Top scorer Mark Hateley hit 22 goals and became the first Englishman to be named 'Player of the Year' by the Scottish Football Writers' Association. In a memorable 'Ne'erday' clash at Celtic Park, the visitors struck like a hurricane and were 3-0 ahead after just half an hour's play. The final 4-2 victory was achieved with goals from Hateley, Alexei Mikhailichenko and Oleg Kuznetsov.

SEASON 1993-94	P	W	D	L	F	A	Pts
Rangers	44	22	14	8	74	41	58
Aberdeen	44	17	21	6	58	36	55
Motherwell	44	20	14	10	58	43	54

SEASON 1994/95

Season 1994/95 saw the Glasgow arrival of Dane Brian Laudrup (an absolute bargain at only £2.25million from Fiorentina of Italy) who would take his place on the Ibrox wall of fame as one of the most talented footballers ever to wear Rangers blue. When Rangers defeated Celtic 3-1 in the league at Hampden in October (Celtic Park was being re-built), Laudrup's goal that afternoon was considered by many to be one of the best of the whole campaign. In total he would net ten times in the 1994/95 period, three short of top scorer Mark Hateley's thirteen strikes in the championship race. Alex McLeish's Motherwell side finished runners-up in the league and Celtic, for the seventh year in succession, finished outside the top two.

SEASON 1994/95	P	W	D	L	F	A	Pts
Rangers	36	20	9	7	60	35	69
Motherwell	36	14	12	10	50	50	54
Hibernian	36	12	17	7	49	37	53

SEASON 1995/96

Paul Gascoigne entered the 1995/96 arena and bleached blonde hair was once again in certain parts of Glasgow. The Old Firm meetings were particularly important that season with a rejuvenated Celtic pushing Rangers all the way. Three of the four Rangers/Celtic clashes were drawn with the Light Blues victorious in the other fixture which was the Parkhead side's only defeat in the title race. In that crucial encounter, goals from full-back Alex Cleland (with a header) and Gascoigne (running virtually the length of the park before netting a McCoist pass for one of the gems of the season) sealed the points. It was the Geordie lad himself who grabbed all the headlines in April when his astonishing hat-trick against Aberdeen finally secured the championship crown for Rangers. Three weeks later at the National Stadium, a crushing 5-1 Scottish Cup final defeat of Hearts meant a domestic double.

SEASON 1995-96	P	W	D	L	F	A	Pts
Rangers	36	27	6	3	85	25	87
Celtic	36	24	11	1	74	25	83
Aberdeen	36	16	7	13	52	45	55

SEASON 1996/97

The final piece of the 'nine' jigsaw was put in place at Tannadice on 7 May 1997. With a rare headed goal - his last was for Fiorentina in a game against Roma - Brian Laudrup secured a 1-0 victory for Rangers and the celebrations began. It was entirely fitting that the Dane's goal should secure the championship as his contribution had once again been quite immense. Not surprisingly, for the second time in just three seasons, the Scottish Football Writers' Association named him Player of the Year. Another 1-0 victory, but this time in the east end of Glasgow in March, had earlier ended Celtic's faint hope of stopping the Rangers juggernaut.

When the first of the sequence had been confirmed back in April 1989, another eight consecutive championships seemed nothing more than an impossible dream.

SEASON 1996/97	P	W	D	L	F	A	Pts
Rangers	36	25	5	6	85	33	80
Celtic	36	23	6	7	78	32	75
Dundee Utd	36	17	9	10	46	33	60

Rangers Managers

William Wilton 1899 - 1920

10 League Championships
& 4 Scottish Cups

Bill Struth 1920 - 1954

18 League Championships,
10 Scottish Cups & 2 League Cups

Scott Symon 1954 - 1967

6 League Championships,
5 Scottish Cups & 4 League Cups

Davie White 1967 - 1969

Willie Waddell 1969 - 1972

1 European Cup Winners' Cup
& 1 League Cup

Jock Wallace 1972 - 1978

3 League Championships,
3 Scottish Cups & 2 League Cups

John Greig 1978 - 1983

2 Scottish Cups & 2 League Cups

Jock Wallace 1983 - 1986

2 League Cups

Graeme Souness 1986 - 1991

3 League Championships
& 4 League Cups

Walter Smith 1991 - 1998

7 League Championships,
3 Scottish Cups & 3 League Cups

Dick Advocaat 1998 - 2001

2 League Championships,
2 Scottish Cups & 1 League Cup

Alex McLeish 2001 - 2006

2 League Championships,
2 Scottish Cups & 3 League Cups

Paul le Guen 2006 - 2007

Walter Smith 2007 - 2011

3 League Championships,
2 Scottish Cups & 3 League Cups

Ally McCoist 2011 - present

ALLY McCOIST: RANGERS LEGEND

SPOT THE BALL

Can you spot which is the real ball?

Answer on Page 61

Lee Wallace

60

QUIZ ANSWERS

RANGERS LEGENDS QUIZ Page 23

1. Jorg Albertz
2. Willie Thornton
3. Terry Butcher
4. Bobby Shearer
5. Graeme Souness
6. Mark Hateley
7. Ray Wilkins
8. Alan Morton
9. Richard Gough
10. Jim Forrest

SPOT THE BALL Page 59

SPOT THE DIFFERENCE Page 29

Where's our mascot, Broxi Bear?
Can you find him in the crowd above?